HAL LEONARD KEYBOARD STYLE SERIES

BOOGIE-WOOGIE PIANO

THE COMPLETE GUIDE WITH AUDIO!

To access audio visit:
www.halleonard.com/mylibrary

Enter Code
3704-4181-5501-0437

BY TODD LOWRY

ISBN 978-1-4803-3031-3

HAL•LEONARD®
CORPORATION
7777 W. BLUEMOUND RD. P.O. BOX 13819 MILWAUKEE, WI 53213

In Australia contact:
Hal Leonard Australia Pty. Ltd.
4 Lentara Court
Cheltenham, Victoria, 3192 Australia
Email: ausadmin@halleonard.com.au

Visit Hal Leonard Online at
www.halleonard.com

INTRODUCTION

Welcome to *Boogie-Woogie Piano*. If you've ever wanted to play in the style of Jools Holland or Dr. John or one of the classic boogie-woogie pianists like Albert Ammons, Pete Johnson, or Meade Lux Lewis, then this book is for you.

Learning how to play boogie-woogie piano is a two-step process. First, you must acquire the basic music vocabulary of the genre. Second, you must spend time practicing at the piano to develop your skills.

This book begins with a general review of the boogie-woogie style and a short chapter devoted to its history. Then we focus on the boogie-woogie harmonic structure and bass line. Later we cover several topics: right-hand techniques; introductions, breaks, and endings; how to play popular melodies in boogie-woogie style; and how to create your own boogie-woogie.

Six complete songs in various boogie-woogies styles are included in the "Style File" chapter at the end of the book. Here, we spotlight the pianistic characteristics of several important boogie-woogie players.

About the Audio

On the accompanying audio, you'll find demonstrations of most of the musical examples in the book. The tracks feature the left-hand part on the left channel, and the right-hand part on the right channel, for easy "hands separate" practice, an important tool for any style of piano playing. The metronome is centered on the tracks, as is the piano when the example is for one hand only. All the musical examples are in 4/4 time. There are four metronome clicks before an example begins. If an example begins on other than beat one, there are additional clicks until the piece begins.

Tracks 1–28 are recorded at the fairly leisurely pace of 100 beats per minute (bpm). Tracks 29–44 are a bit faster, at 120 bpm. Tracks 45–55 are recorded at an even faster 140 bpm. The songs in the Style File are each recorded twice: once at a slow pace of 100 bpm and once at a typical boogie-woogie tempo, either 160 or 170 bpm. Boogie-woogies sometimes reach speeds as high as 200 bpm or more.

About the Author

Todd Lowry has written several keyboard instructional books for Hal Leonard Corporation, including *Best of Blues Piano*, *Today's Piano Greats*, and *New Orleans Piano Styles*. A former staff arranger for Hal Leonard, he created hundreds of music folios, including *The Complete Beatles*. In his varied career, Todd has been music supervisor at a major theme park, the music critic for a major daily newspaper, and a working jazz pianist. His arrangements have appeared on a Grammy-nominated album. He lives in Albuquerque, New Mexico.

Websites of Interest

www.boogiewoogie.com
www.boogiewoogiemarshall.com
www.boogiewoogiepiano.net
www.bowofo.org
www.colindavey.com

CONTENTS

Chapter 1
WHAT IS BOOGIE-WOOGIE PIANO?

Boogie-woogie is a piano style that became popular in the 1930s, but its origins date back to the 19th century. Although it reached its height of popularity in the 1940s, it has etched a permanent place in the piano music field and has maintained its popularity over decades.

The most characteristic feature of boogie-woogie is its use of forceful, repetitive bass figures in the left hand. The repetition of these bass patterns gives boogie-woogie its unique drive and gave rise to the term "eight to the bar," since the bass patterns usually contain eight eighth notes per measure. The bass patterns are normally one or two measures in length.

The function of the boogie-woogie bass line is two-fold: it establishes and maintains the basic beat of the piece and, at the same time, forms a harmonic background for whatever is being played by the right hand.

For the most part, boogie-woogie tunes are 12-bar blues. However, the style has been applied to popular, non-blues songs like Stephen Foster's "Old Folks at Home" (Swanee River) and hymns such as "Just a Closer Walk with Thee."

The 12-bar blues pattern is the most common structure in all of Western pop music. It is the basis of most blues, boogie-woogies, and early rock 'n' roll songs. It consists of a 12-measure chord pattern. The chords are built on the root (1st), the 4th, or the 5th degrees of the scale. All three of these chords are usually played as dominant 7th chords. We refer to these as the I7, IV7, and V7 chords. (We discuss the harmonic structure of boogie-woogie in Chapter 3.)

Boogie-woogies can be in any key, but a great deal of them are written in the key of C. Some of the greatest boogie-woogie practitioners never played outside that key, and a large proportion of the musical examples in this book are also in C major.

For proper interpretation of boogie-woogie, you must understand the difference between *straight*-eighth notes and *swing*-eighth notes. Eighth notes are played differently depending on the style of music being performed. Most boogie-woogies use *swung* eighth notes. That is to say, the second of each pair of eighth notes is played on the last *third* of the beat rather than on the midpoint between beats. The underlying triplet feel is central to what we call "swing."

Think of a series of swing-eighth notes as a series of triplets with the first two notes of each triplet tied together. That's how swing-eighth notes should be played:

Boogie-woogie sheet music used to be written with dotted-eighth and 16th notes:

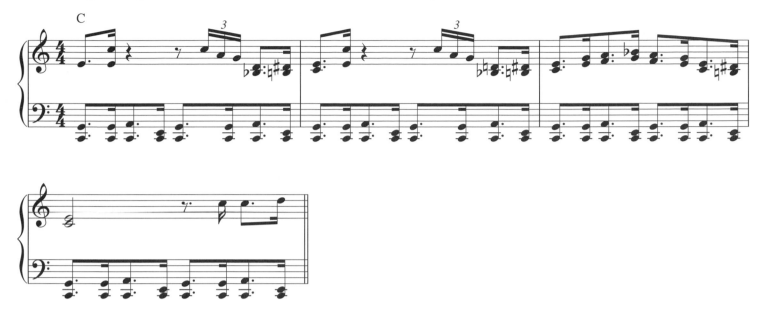

This rhythm is not correct, though, because boogie-woogie has a swung, triplet feel. Sometimes boogie-woogie sheet music is written with triplets:

While this rhythm is accurate, the notation is cumbersome and overly complicated. Therefore, we have chosen to write all the boogie-woogies in this book with the understanding that all eighth notes are to be played swing-style:

The meter of boogie-woogie is, with rare exceptions, either 4/4 or cut-time. It is a percussive sort of music and the sustain pedal is seldom used or not used at all. Boogie-woogie nearly always features a moderate to fast tempo. To practice, one should start by playing slowly and gradually increase the speed. A metronome is useful for this. (See "About the Audio" on page 2.)

The right-hand part in a boogie-woogie is usually made up of short, repeated phrases called "riffs." The right hand often features sequential patterns, tonal repetitions, polyrhythms, and devices such as tremolos and tone clusters. The right-hand figurations over the steady figures in the left hand often create cross rhythms.

Boogie-woogie is sometimes confused with ragtime. Ragtime is a solo piano style characterized by syncopation in the right hand and by "oom-pah" rhythms in the left hand, i.e., bass notes on beats 1 and 3 of the measure and chords on beats 2 and 4. It is most associated with composer Scott Joplin, and was being published by the late 1890s.

Boogie-woogie is also sometimes confused with stride piano. Stride is a form of jazz piano with the same sort of "oom-pah" bass lines as ragtime music. Practitioners of stride include Fats Waller, James P. Johnson, and Eubie Blake.

Though boogie-woogie is usually performed as solo piano music, big bands adapted it in the 1940s and the Spirituals to Swing concerts of 1938–39 included group boogie-woogie performances.

The origin of the term "boogie-woogie" is unknown. However, Dr. John Tennison, a San Antonio psychiatrist, pianist, musicologist, and founder of The Boogie-Woogie Foundation, has suggested some interesting linguistic connections with African terms. There is the Hausa word "Boog" and the Mandingo word "Booga," both of which mean "to beat," as in beating a drum. There is also the West African word "Bogi," which means "to dance," and the Bantu term "Mbuki Mvuki," which means to take off in flight and to dance wildly. The meanings of these words are generally consistent with the characteristics of boogie-woogie music, and their African origin is consistent with the fact that the music originated among African-Americans.

Chapter 2
THE HISTORY OF BOOGIE-WOOGIE PIANO

Because it is usually based on the 12-bar blues pattern, boogie-woogie is fundamentally connected with the blues. However, boogie-woogie possesses a musical language of its own and there are major differences between the two styles.

In the beginning, blues was primarily a vocal idiom. It originated out of the call-and-response patterns of African tribal music. The evolution of the blues continued in the field hollers, work songs, and spirituals sung by African-American slaves and their descendants in the southern United States.

Blues, in its various moods, traditionally depicts the emotions of sadness and sorrow. The blues is usually in a slow tempo and on a moderate dynamic level. On the other hand, boogie-woogie is an instrumental style usually fast and loud. It transmits a raw, buoyant energy. Full of vitality and excitement, boogie-woogie expresses an exuberance of spirit. It was originally associated with dancing and fun. No other kind of piano music is so infectious.

In addition to his research into the origin of the term "boogie-woogie," Dr. John Tennison has made inquiries into the geographical origins of boogie-woogie. Oral histories from the 1930s revealed a broad consensus that boogie-woogie was first played in the Piney Woods of northeast Texas in the 1870s. It is agreed that boogie-woogie piano players were first heard in the lumber and turpentine camps, remote rural work camps where large numbers of African-American laborers were employed.

With the lumber and turpentine camps came "barrelhouses" – taverns where liquor was sold from big wooden barrels. A barrelhouse was often set up in a simple cabin or under canvas. A row of three or four barrels would be covered with planks to form a bar. Barrelhouses featured gambling, dancing, hard drinking, and general hell-raising for the amusement of the tough workers who made up the clientele. They were rough places. It was not uncommon that during a weekend a worker got killed in a liquor-fueled fight over gambling or women.

Pianos, often castoffs, occupied the center of entertainment in these rundown honky-tonks. The pianos were subject to changes in humidity, weekend beer baths, and cigarette burns. Piano players traveled on the barrelhouse circuit. Since these pianists had no instrument to carry, it was easy for them to hop a train and roam from camp to camp or from town to town looking for a place to play. The reception they were accorded determined the duration of their stay at any barrelhouse.

Most of these wandering pianists ultimately vanished, leaving behind no written records or audio recordings, only their colorful names: Kid Stormy Weather, Barrelhouse Welch, Jack the Bear, Drive 'Em Down, No Leg Kenny, and the list goes on.

Piano players in the barrelhouse didn't tickle the ivories. They smashed them. Pianists had to develop an aggressive, rhythmic style to be heard above the crowd and to keep pace with the rowdy atmosphere. The trick was to make themselves heard and the best way to do that was to play loud. These self-taught boogie-woogie pioneers created a pianistic language suitable to the rough audience and the dilapidated instruments. That's how the boogie-woogie style developed. It was a form of dance music meant to be rhythmic, fast, and loud.

Barrelhouse piano included an eclectic mixture of styles. Influences from ragtime, stride, and blues all appeared in the early forms of boogie-woogie. It is agreed that "Fast Western" or "Fast Blues" was the term by which boogie-woogie was known around 1900.

Jazz pioneer Jelly Roll Morton recalled hearing boogie-woogie played when he was a child (in the 1890s). Morton said that, in those days, it was called "Honky-Tonk" or "Texas Style."

In 2010, Dr. Tennison summarized his research into the origins of boogie-woogie with the conclusion that Marshall, Texas is the geographical center of gravity for instances of boogie-woogie performance between 1870 and 1880. The municipality now calls itself "The Birthplace of Boogie-Woogie."

The 1919 recordings (in two takes) of "Weary Blues" by the Louisiana Five were the earliest sound recordings that contain a boogie-woogie bass figure, according to Tennison. The first boogie-woogie piano solo record is generally considered to be Jimmy Blythe's recording of "Chicago Stomps" from April 1924.

The first modern-day spelling of boogie-woogie was used by Clarence "Pinetop" Smith in his December 1928 recording titled "Pinetop's Boogie-Woogie." The song's lyrics were instructions on how to dance to the tune. Released in 1929, "Pinetop's Boogie-Woogie" was also the first boogie-woogie recording to be a commercial hit. It was closely followed by "Honky-Tonk Train Blues" by Meade Lux Lewis, recorded in 1927 and released in 1930.

In the 1920s, many African-Americans in the South migrated to the industrial centers of the North to find better jobs and escape the prejudices below the Mason-Dixon Line. Many barrelhouse and blues pianists made the move north. Kansas City, St. Louis, and especially Chicago became urban centers for blues and boogie-woogie. These pianists often took menial jobs as taxi drivers and dish washers. They supplemented their income by playing at rent parties in the evenings or weekends. In urban centers, rent parties were popular. By charging admission to a party in his apartment, a tenant was able to keep a roof over his head. These events offered food, bootleg liquor, and music for dancing

The first generation of boogie-woogie pianists includes those active up to about 1930. Among these were: Hersal Thomas, composer of the influential piece "The Fives," who died of poisoning at age 17; Charles "Cow Cow" Davenport, composer of "Cow Cow Blues," who was expelled from Alabama Theological Seminary for "ragging" a march; Little Brother Montgomery, composer of "Vicksburg Blues;" "Cripple" Clarence Lofton, who used a walking bass and played only in the keys of C and G. Others include Roosevelt Sykes, Montana Taylor, Rufus "Speckled Red" Perryman, Pinetop Smith, and Jimmy Yancey.

Clarence "Pinetop" Smith (1904–1929) was born and raised in Alabama. He received his nickname from his penchant as a boy for climbing trees. He moved to Chicago in 1928 to record his music. "Pinetop's Boogie-Woogie," recorded in 1928, is perhaps the single most important and influential boogie-woogie composition of all time. Its distinctive melodic motives have been used time and time again in boogie-woogie, blues, and rock 'n' roll compositions. It was arranged for big band and recorded by the Tommy Dorsey Orchestra in 1938.

For a time, Pinetop lived in the same apartment building as two other boogie-woogie pianists, Albert Ammons and Meade Lux Lewis. The three would meet at Ammons's apartment, the only one that had a piano. Pinetop taught Ammons his "Pinetop's Boogie-Woogie" and Ammons later recorded it under the title "Boogie-Woogie Stomp." Pinetop died tragically in 1929 when he was hit by a stray bullet during a fight in a Chicago dance hall the day before he was due to return to the studio to record his second session.

Another major Chicago pianist was Jimmy Yancey (1894–1951). Yancey was a noted pianist by 1915. He was close to both Ammons and Lewis, although he later had a legal dispute with Lewis over the song "Yancey Special." For 30 years, Yancey supported himself working as a groundskeeper for the Chicago White Sox at Comiskey Park. He was a big influence on both Ammons and Lewis. Part of his style was that he played in a variety of keys, but ended every song in E-flat. Yancey was inducted into the Rock and Roll Hall of Fame in 1986.

The second generation of boogie-woogie performers carried the music forward between 1930 and the late 1940s. These include Ammons, Lewis, and Pete Johnson from Kansas City. The three joined forces in 1938 and became known as the Boogie-Woogie Trio.

Albert Ammons (1907–1949) was born and lived in Chicago. He learned from piano rolls and records and was influenced by Jimmy Yancey. He never learned how to read music, but could play in different keys and transpose. His most important recordings include "Monday Struggle" and "Boogie-Woogie Stomp."

Like Ammons, Meade Lux Lewis (1905–1964) was born and lived in Chicago. He recorded the legendary "Honky-Tonk Train Blues" in 1927. He got his inspiration from the Big Bertha locomotives that passed his house several times a day. Ammons and Lewis were close friends and worked together at the Silver Taxicab Company. The owner of the cab company cleverly installed a piano in the driver's dispatch office so he could be sure to find a driver there when a taxi was needed.

Pete Johnson (1904–1967) was born in Kansas City and played drums professionally before taking up the piano. Johnson formed a collaboration with blues shouter Joe Turner. Johnson's most famous composition is "Roll 'Em Pete" which he used to accompany Turner's improvised lyrics. Other Pete Johnson compositions include "Death Ray Boogie" and "Dive Bomber."

Music producer and talent scout John Hammond (1910–1987), who discovered Billie Holliday – and later discovered Bob Dylan, Aretha Franklin, and Bruce Springsteen – became fascinated with boogie-woogie in 1928 after hearing a recording of "Pinetop's Boogie-Woogie." Later, in 1931, after he heard a recording of "Honky-Tonk Train Blues," he sought out Meade Lux Lewis. It took Hammond several years to find Lewis – in 1935, working in a Chicago car wash.

In 1938, Hammond put together the first Spirituals to Swing Concert in New York City's Carnegie Hall. Ammons, Lewis, and Johnson first came together for this performance. They played solos, duets, and trios and accompanied Joe Turner on some songs. Thus, boogie-woogie had transcended its original function as dance music to become a listening experience, pure concert music. The enthusiastic reception for the event marked the beginning of the boogie-woogie craze. Record producer Alfred Lion attended the show. Two weeks later, he started Blue Note Records, recording nine Ammons solos and eight by Lewis, along with a pair of duets.

The Boogie-Woogie Trio became international stars and in 1939 began a two-year engagement at Café Society, a Greenwich Village club. It was the first racially integrated New York nightspot, as boogie-woogie became fashionable among New York socialites. The Boogie-Woogie Trio performances were regularly broadcast on the radio. Lewis, Johnson, and Ammons became the most famous pianists of the time. Ammons played at President Harry S. Truman's inauguration celebration, while Lewis appeared in the movie *It's a Wonderful Life*, playing piano in the scene where George Bailey gets thrown out of Nick's Bar.

During the boogie-woogie craze, all the big bands – Benny Goodman, Count Basie, Woody Herman, Harry James, Tommy Dorsey, Lionel Hampton, and others – recorded boogie-woogies. Boogie-woogie arrangements of popular tunes began to appear. The Andrews Sisters became immensely popular singing "The Boogie-Woogie Bugle Boy of Company B" and other boogie-style hits.

This boogie-woogie craze lasted throughout the 1940s. Eventually, kitschy songs (such as "Chopsticks Boogie" and "Chopin's Polonaise in Boogie") replaced much of what had been an innovative piano style. By the end of the 1940s, public interest in boogie-woogie began to wane. It slipped out of public favor, a victim of dilution, commercial exploitation, and overexposure. Boogie-woogie was a victim of its own success.

Musical opportunities for Lewis and Johnson were reduced to almost nothing. (Ammons had died in 1949.) Lewis switched from playing boogie-woogie to playing standards. There was very little work. He scraped by until 1964, when he died in a car accident in Minneapolis after a gig. Johnson had bad luck, too. He resorted to menial jobs such as washing cars. An accident in 1952 sliced off part of one of his fingers and a stroke in 1958 left him partly paralyzed. His last years were troubled by illness and poverty.

While the commercialization of boogie-woogie spelled an end to the boogie-woogie craze, the genre had a major influence on the emerging style of rock 'n' roll, especially on Little Richard, Fats Domino, Jerry Lee Lewis, and Johnnie Johnson, who played piano with Chuck Berry. It became a standard element in the blues pianist's repertoire and also influenced country music through the songs of Western Swing pioneer Bob Wills and subsequent country artists such as Asleep at the Wheel.

Boogie-woogie began as a music played by African-American males, first in Southern barrelhouses and then in Midwestern cities such as Chicago, Kansas City, and St. Louis. In the 1940s there were some notable female practitioners, including Mary Lou Williams and Hazel Scott. Boogie-woogie crossed over to the white audience and white musicians began to play it. Today, boogie-woogie is a democratic music, crossing all boundaries of class, race, sex, age, and location.

The majority of today's boogie-woogie pianists are white, including a large contingent of European pianists. A fair number of practitioners are women. Besides the United States, there are notable players in Canada and Japan, as well as in the European countries of Germany, France, the Netherlands, Austria, Sweden, Switzerland, Spain, Belgium, and England.

Public interest in boogie-woogie today is international in scope. The very first international boogie-woogie festival was held in 1974 in Cologne, Germany. Currently there are international festivals in Salzburg, Austria; Dorset, England; Laroquebrou, France; Beaune, France; Lugano, Switzerland; Barcelona, Spain; Kitzbühel, Austria; and Ermelo, Holland. Boogie-woogie is being taken forward by such international pianists as Michael Kaeshammer, Rob Rio, Sivan Zingg, and Axel Zwingenberger.

In 2012, the ensemble known as "The A, B, C and D of Boogie-Woogie" played sold-out shows and brought boogie-woogie to a new generation of fans. The group is made up of Axel Zwingenberger on piano, Ben Waters on piano, Charlie Watts (from the Rolling Stones) on drums, and Dave Green on bass.

Chapter 3

THE HARMONIC STRUCTURE OF THE BOOGIE-WOOGIE

The construction of the boogie-woogie is usually based on the 12-bar blues pattern, the most common structure in all of Western pop music. The pattern is repeated several times during the boogie-woogie. Each 12-bar section is called a chorus.

The 12-bar blues pattern is built around three chords – the tonic (I), subdominant (IV), and dominant (V) of the key. In C major, these chords are C, F, and G. Often, all three chords are in a dominant 7th form.

Measures 11 and 12 of the form are a turnaround section leading back to the beginning of the form or leading to an ending in the final Chorus. Here is a 12-bar blues structure in the key of C major:

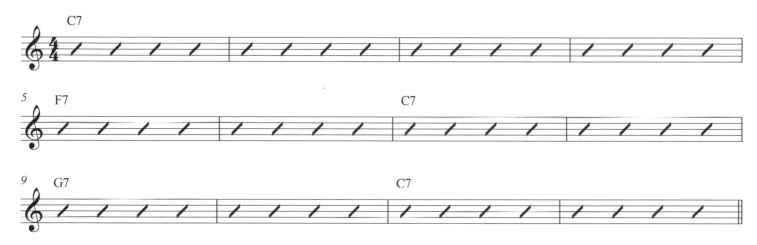

Sometimes the chords of measures 2 and 10 are replaced by the subdominant (IV) chord. We'll call this the 12-bar blues, version two:

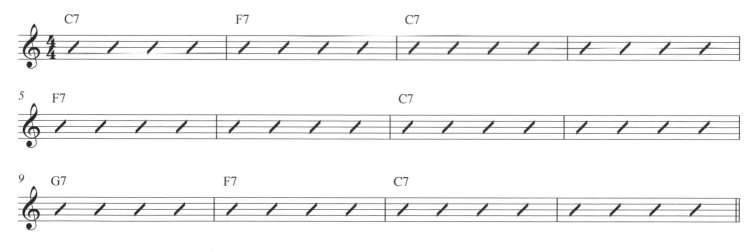

In general, boogie-woogie uses the first form of the 12-bar blues, but sometimes the second form is used for contrast.

It is useful to know the 12-bar blues in as many keys as possible. Here, for your reference, is the 12-bar blues (version one) in the commonly used keys of F major and G major:

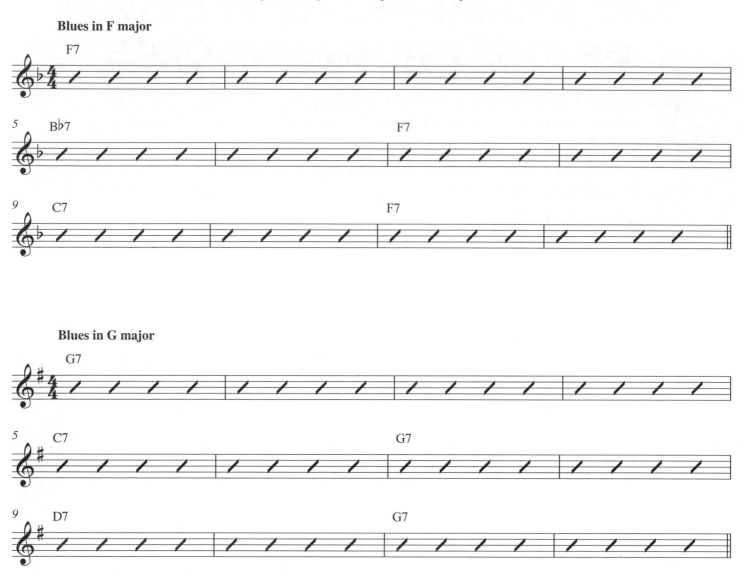

Blues in F major

Blues in G major

The exception to the use of the 12-bar blues pattern for a boogie-woogie is when the piece is based on a pre-existing tune, such as a pop song or a classical piece. An example is "Swanee River Boogie" based on Stephen Foster's "Old Folks at Home," otherwise known as "Swanee River." In this case, the older song provides the harmonic structure. It so happens that "Old Folks at Home" is a 32-measure song that uses the chords I, IV, and V, the same three chords as the 12-bar blues. Here is the harmonic structure of "Swanee River Boogie."

Chapter 4
THE BOOGIE-WOOGIE BASS LINE

The left-hand bass line is the most characteristic feature of boogie-woogie, providing the rhythmic and harmonic foundation. The object is to play the bass line with precision, speed, and stamina. The key to this is repetitious practice. You must practice until you can play the bass line automatically. The groove must be solid. Your left hand should be on auto-pilot so that you can focus on the different right-hand techniques we'll be looking at.

Most boogie-woogie bass lines consist of a one- or two-measure figure, with each measure containing eight eighth notes. As noted in Chapter 1, this is where the term "eight to the bar" comes from. In general, a boogie-woogie piece keeps the same bass line going throughout the entire piece. There are exceptions, however – most notably, "Boogie-Woogie Stomp" and "Shout for Joy" by Albert Ammons.

There are two kinds of boogie-woogie bass lines: standing and walking. In standing bass lines, the left hand stays in one position for each chord. In walking bass lines, the left hand generally changes position on each beat. Standing bass lines are used more often than walking bass lines in boogie-woogie.

There are three kinds of standing bass lines:

• single-note lines
• double-note lines
• chordal lines

Single-Note Bass Lines

Single-note bass lines are made up of single eighth notes. The following are typical boogie-woogie single-note bass figures. Each example is played twice on the audio.

14

Next, we'll apply two of these patterns to the 12-bar blues progression. Example A is the bass line to "Swanee River Boogie" as played by Albert Ammons in the key of C. Example B is the bass line to "Boogie-Woogie" by Pete Johnson in the key of G.

Practice single-note bass lines using the 12-bar blues progression. Use a metronome or drum machine until the groove is solid.

Double-Note Bass Lines

Double-note bass lines contain two-note intervals, as well as single notes. The following are signature double-note bass lines. Each example is played twice on the audio.

Examples (j) – (m) are the kind of double-note bass lines favored by contemporary German pianist Axel Zwingenberger.

Next, we'll apply one of these double-note bass patterns to the 12-bar blues chord progression. Track 4 is the bass line to "Pinetop's Boogie-Woogie" by Pinetop Smith in the key of C major.

C Blues

Practice double-note bass patterns using the 12-bar blues progression. Use a metronome or drum machine until the groove is solid.

Chordal Bass Lines

Chordal bass lines are made up of triads or more complex chords. The chordal bass line was particularly favored by Meade Lux Lewis.

The following examples are chordal bass lines; each is played twice. Examples (a) and (c) are taken from "Honky Tonk Train Blues" by Meade Lux Lewis. Example (b) comes from his song "Yancey Goes Honky Tonk."

TRACK 5

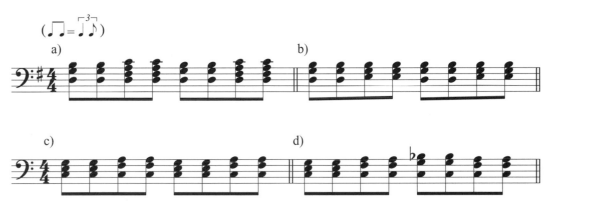

These patterns are denser than the single- and double-notes lines. You'll want to avoid playing them too low on the piano, because they'll sound muddy.

Next, we've applied a 12-bar blues progression in the key of G to the "Honky Tonk Train Blues" chordal bass line. Notice that the pattern doesn't transpose exactly from one chord to another. For example, the G chord is played with a D in the bass, while the C chord is played with a C in the bass. The D7 chord is played with a D in the bass and simply alternates between D and D7.

TRACK 6

Walking Bass Lines

The boogie-woogie walking bass line is comprised of broken octaves in eighth notes, typically outlining the arpeggio of a chord – usually a triad, a sixth chord, or a dominant 7th chord. The left hand changes position with each beat of the bass line. Walking bass lines look like this; each is played twice on the audio:

TRACK 7

Now, we'll apply one of these patterns to the 12-bar blues progression in the key of C:

TRACK 8

New bass lines can be derived by combining part of one figure with part of another. For instance, the first half of one figure can be combined with the first or second half of another figure.

Probably the most difficult part of playing boogie-woogie is coordinating the right hand with the left hand. Before any attempt is made at playing the hands simultaneously, they must be made completely independent of each other. The bass line should be mastered with the left hand so that it can be played in strict time with a swing feel and without the distraction of concentrating on the notes in the bass figure. Do not attempt to play both hands together until you have mastered the bass figure. Many bass figures are quite difficult to play and may take considerable practice.

Here's how to play a boogie-woogie bass line:

- Select a bass line to learn.

- Figure out a fingering that fits your hand.

- Practice the line in its tonic (I) position.

- Practice the line in its subdominant (IV) and dominant (V) positions.

- Practice the line in a 12-bar blues progression.

- Practice several choruses in a row until you can play ten consecutive choruses.

- Practice the line using the 12-bar blues (version two) progression.

- Practice until you can play it comfortably. It should become automatic.

Chapter 5
THE RIGHT HAND – RHYTHMIC CHORDAL PATTERNS

Most boogie-woogies have at least one chorus in which the right-hand part consists of chords in repeated rhythmic patterns. In "Pinetop's Boogie-Woogie" the right-hand rhythmic chordal pattern is as follows:

TRACK 9

The next two exercises represent chordal choruses over two different bass lines. The purpose is to get used to playing with both hands, maintaining the boogie-woogie bass line in the left hand and playing something fairly simple in the right hand. Before you play both hands together, learn the bass line in each exercise separately.

Start by practicing the exercises slowly, gradually working up the speed. By practicing these exercises, your left hand will be getting more automatic so that you can focus your attention on the right hand.

Track 10 showcases the bass line of "Pinetop's Boogie-Woogie":

TRACK 10

Track 11 uses the bass line found in both "Shout for Joy" and "Monday Struggle" by Albert Ammons:

As we progress through the exercises in the rest of the book, here are some tips to help your progress:

• Try to memorize as much as you can. Practice without the sheet music in front of you.

• Record yourself frequently to check on your sound and your progress.

• As often as you can, listen to recordings by boogie-woogie pianists. The best way to learn to play boogie-woogie piano is by imitation. You are unlikely to become a good boogie-woogie pianist without listening to and studying the masters.

• Try out ideas of your own.

Chapter 6
THE RIGHT HAND –
MELODIC RIFFS

The right hand of most boogie-woogies is built out of one- or two-bars riffs. These riffs are then repeated, combined, and varied within the boogie-woogie structure. Let's analyze some of these riffs.

Figures based on parallel 3rds are common in boogie-woogie. The 3rds can move in ascending or descending order. Normally, the 3rds resolve into the chord they're played over. The phrases below all resolve into a C major chord. Practice developing your own phrases using 3rds.

TRACK 12

Figures based on parallel 6ths are common in boogie-woogie. The 6ths can move in ascending or descending order. Normally, the 6ths resolve into the chord they're played over. The phrases below all resolve into a C chord. Practice developing your own phrases in 6ths.

TRACK 13

Now we will integrate the 3rds and 6ths interval techniques to create a right-hand solo over a 12-bar blues progression in C with a bass line based on Pete Johnson's "Boogie-Woogie."

Two-beat descending riffs similar to those in Track 15 are common in boogie-woogie. The first half-beat is a single note, interval, or chord. The rest of the pattern forms a descending figure, with the second half-beat in 16th notes, 16th note triplets, or 32nd notes. The second beat consists of two eighth notes. Practice developing your own phrases. Each pattern is played twice on the audio:

TRACK 15

Figures containing repeated notes are common in boogie-woogie. These repeated notes can be single notes, octaves, 3rds, other intervals, or repeated chords. Repetition is one of the most important and easiest ways to improvise.

TRACK 16

Let's put the combination of two-beat riffs and repeated notes to work in the following right-hand solo over the 12-bar C blues progression, with a boogie-woogie left hand in a standard pattern:

Blues riffs are common in boogie-woogie. Following are some examples:

Note that, in boogie-woogie, the major blues scale is more commonly used. In the key of C, this is C-D-E♭-E-G-A-C:

Major Blues Scale – Key of C

TRACK 19

The minor blues scale – C-E♭-F-F♯-G-B♭-C in the key of C – often sounds too dark for the exuberant nature of boogie-woogie:

Minor Blues Scale – Key of C

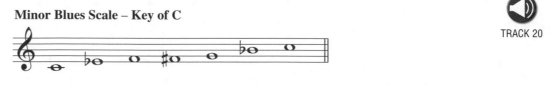

TRACK 20

Descending pentatonic scale runs are common in boogie-woogies. These use the C major pentatonic and C minor pentatonic scales:

C Major Pentatonic Scale

TRACK 21

C Minor Pentatonic Scale

Drone notes are common in boogie-woogies. A drone note is a repeated note above or below a moving line or phrase. Following are some examples. Notice that, in most cases, the tonic (I) is the drone note:

TRACK 22

Now let's use blues riffs, pentatonic scale runs, and drone notes in a right-hand solo with a standard boogie-woogie bass line:

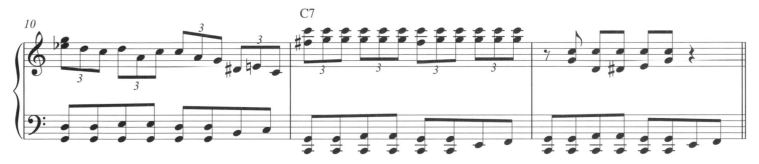

An indispensable part of the boogie-woogie vocabulary is the crossover right-hand lick, what Dr. John has called "the famous lick." The licks below work over a C or C7 chord. These are especially effective in boogie-woogie when played in measure 11 of the 12-bar blues form. All the examples are basically variations on the same lick.

TRACK 24

Now let's combine a variety of crossover licks to create a right-hand solo over the C blues progression with a standard boogie-woogie bass line:

TRACK 25

Chapter 7

THE MELODIC LINE –
SPECIAL TECHNIQUES

Grace Notes/Crushed Notes

A grace note is an ornamentation of a melody tone. Grace notes are sometimes referred to as "crushed notes." Whereas the human voice, stringed instruments, and wind instruments can bend a tone by sliding it sharp or flat, the piano is made up of 88 discrete notes. Thus, we use grace notes in boogie-woogie to imitate bent notes or "blue notes," which are sung or played at a slightly lower pitch than that of the major scale – for expressive purposes. The blue notes are the flatted 3rd, the flatted 5th, and the flatted 7th degrees of the scale:

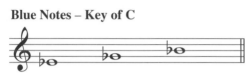

Blue Notes – Key of C

In boogie-woogie, grace notes are usually played on the beat, crushed into the melody tone, as in Example A below:

TRACK 26

Most frequently, grace notes are applied either by half step or whole step from *below* the melody note. However, it is entirely possible to have a grace note applied from *above* the melody note, as shown in Example B above. Grace notes are often combined with 3rds or other intervals, as in Example C. As in Example D, grace notes may be applied to a chord. Often, grace notes consist of several consecutive tones crushed into the melody tone, as in Example E.

In boogie-woogie, the same finger is generally used on a grace note to slide into the melody tone, like Example F. Because one can't slide with the same finger from one white key to another or from a white key to a black key, sometimes two fingers are necessary to perform the grace note and the melody note; see Example G. It's possible to have two or three grace notes when one is playing an interval or a chord, as demonstrated in Example H.

Tremolos

A tremolo is a rapid oscillation between two distinct tones or combinations of tones. On the piano, a quick rocking motion between fingers of one hand produces the tremolo. Tremolos can consist of an octave, of smaller intervals, or of whole chords. Tremolos occur frequently in boogie-woogie.

To play a tremolo, pick an interval larger than a whole step and alternate playing the two (or more) notes as quickly as possible. The graphic notation of a tremolo indicates that your fingers are rolling between the two (or more) notes, as shown in Example A:

Tremolos occur frequently on 3rds, 6ths or octaves; see Example B above. Sometimes a tremolo consists of a whole chord; F major and C7 are shown in Example C. Tremolos can also be performed with both hands, like the C7 chord in Example D. Tremolos can be combined with other ornamentations. Example E is a classic figure – a tremolo on the interval of a 3rd embellished with two grace notes

Try inserting tremolos into your playing for more variety.

Glissandos

A glissando (abbreviated as *gliss.*) is a slide or glide on the piano keys. It can either ascend or descend. Descending glissandos are more common. Glissandos can either be on the white keys or the black keys of the piano. White key glissandos are more common.

To perform a descending glissando, place the thumbnail of your right hand on a high white note with your thumbnail facing left and drag your thumb down from right to left across the keys toward the lower keys.

To perform an ascending glissando, place the nail of your right middle finger on a low white note with the nail facing right and drag your finger up from left to right across the keys towards the top of the keyboard.

When you perform glissandos, make sure that only your fingernails touch the keys because it's easy to break your cuticle if you drag skin across the keys.

The example below shows how a glissando is notated – with the abbreviation *gliss.* and a wavy line going from the note you start on to approximately the note you end on. Both ascending and descending glissandos are performed on Track 28.

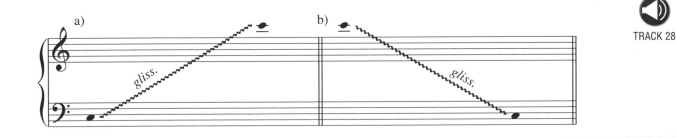

Clusters

The boogie-woogie pianist sometimes strikes simultaneously two (or more) notes situated a whole-step or half-step apart. This is called a tone cluster and adds excitement to the inherent drive of the boogie-woogie.

Meade Lux Lewis had a particular fondness for tone clusters. At times, these created quite a dissonant sound. Following are some examples of clusters used in boogie-woogie. Sometimes the lowest two notes in the right hand must be played with the thumb.

TRACK 29

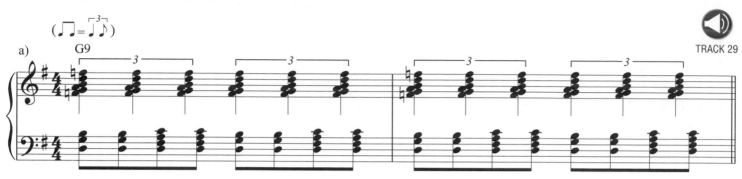

Intentional Dissonance

Sometimes both the major 3rd and minor 3rd of a chord are played simultaneously, for an intentionally dissonant sound.

TRACK 30

Chapter 8

THE RIGHT HAND – DEVELOPING THE MELODIC RIFF

We discovered in Chapter 6 how boogie-woogie right-hand melodic riffs are constructed – out of parallel 3rds, parallel 6ths, two-beat riffs, repeated notes, blues riffs, and drone notes. In Chapter 7 we learned special right-hand techniques – grace notes, tremolos, glissandos, tone clusters, and intentional dissonance. This chapter discusses how melodic riffs can be developed into a complete 12-bar melody.

First, a riff can simply be repeated verbatim several times over the 12-bar blues progression. The example below does this, taking a riff similar to one in "Pinetop's Boogie-Woogie." The riff is repeated note-for-note ten times, except for slight modifications of the accidentals to allow the riff to fit the chords of the blues progression. Bars 11 and 12, the turnaround section, feature a crossover lick in C.

TRACK 31

Playing the riff in sequence is another technique of melodic development. A sequence occurs when a motive is repeated at a higher or lower pitch level. Here's the "Pinetop"-like riff played in sequence, i.e., the riff is transposed to match the chords of the 12-bar blues progression:

TRACK 32

Rhythmic augmentation of the riff, lengthening the note values, is a further technique. The riff in Track 33 is similar to one in "Roll 'Em Pete." The riff is repeated once, then augmented rhythmically, with the eighth notes becoming quarter notes:

TRACK 33

One can also use rhythmic diminution, shortening the rhythmic values. Here, the eighth notes morph into a faster triplet figure:

TRACK 34

Rhythmic displacement is a technique in which the notes of the riff are the same, but the riff starts in a different place in the bar:

TRACK 35

One can fragment the riff, breaking it apart into smaller fragments:

TRACK 36

Notes can be omitted. In this example, based upon a riff found in "Monday Struggle," notes are progressively left out:

TRACK 37

Notes can also be added. Here, with the use of a triplet figure, two notes become three:

TRACK 38

Intervals can be expanded or contracted:

TRACK 39

A motive can be inverted (turned upside down):

TRACK 40

A riff can be played in retrograde (backward):

TRACK 41

One can embellish the riff with ornamentation:

Finally, we can take a page from jazz players and use a musical quote from another song in the melody. I once heard a pianist play a bit of Danny Elfman's "The Theme from *The Simpsons*" in a boogie-woogie improvisation. It was both funny and clever.

Here is a summary of motivic development techniques:

- Literal repetition

- Repeat in sequence

- Rhythmic augmentation

- Rhythmic diminution

- Rhythmic displacement

- Fragmentation

- Omit notes

- Add notes

- Change intervals (expand or contract)

- Inversion

- Retrograde

- Ornamentation

- Quotation

Track 43 demonstrates motivic development techniques, using a common boogie-woogie riff over a classic single-note bass line. It is a two-chorus boogie-woogie in the key of C and begins with a four-bar introduction. (Intros are discussed in Chapter 10.)

The first chorus features a two-bar riff that is then repeated with added notes. The riff is repeated literally in its original version over the IV chord and then played again with added notes and rhythmic diminution.

The second chorus features a new riff, which is then repeated. A secondary riff in bars 19 and 20 answers the first one. The first riff recurs in sequence over the IV chord. The riff is varied for the remainder of the chorus. The piece draws to a close with a stock ending. (Endings are discussed in Chapter 10.)

TRACK 43

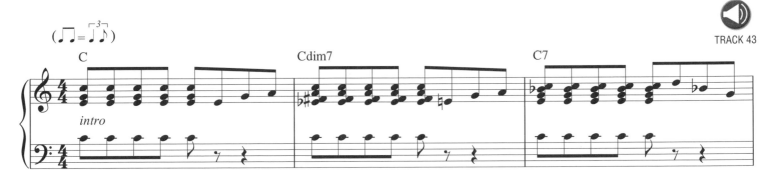

Chapter 9

USING THE 12-BAR BLUES PATTERN, VERSION TWO

Remember that there are two versions of the basic 12-bar blues. The 12-bar blues pattern, version two, has a IV chord (F in the key of C) in bars 2 and 10. Most boogie-woogies use the 12-bar blues, version one, but version two is occasionally used to create variety.

Below is a right-hand melody over the 12-bar blues, version two, in the key of C. Note that in bars 2 and 10 where there is a IV7 chord (F7 in the key of C), the right-hand melody is modified note-wise to coincide with the chord changes. As a matter of practice, you can change any 12-bar blues version one to a version two for variety's sake.

TRACK 44

Chapter 10

INTRODUCTIONS, TURNAROUNDS, ENDINGS, AND BREAKS

Introductions

There are several ways to begin a boogie-woogie. First, you can simply start the boogie-woogie on measure 1 of the chorus with both hands. Second, you can play a bass line for several measures before the right hand joins in. When the right hand joins in, it's measure 1 of the first chorus. This is how "Swanee River Boogie" usually starts. Third, you can play an introduction.

In boogie-woogie, an introduction is usually not in boogie-woogie style. The most common is four measures of material starting on the tonic (I), followed by measure 5 of the chorus. Thus, the introduction is played instead of the first four measures of the chorus.

A common technique is to play the tonic chord in measure 1, the tonic in diminished 7th form in measure 2, and the tonic in dominant 7th form in measures 3 and 4 with a descending figure in the right hand. In effect, there's a tonic pedal point present in all chords of the introduction. Here is an example of that sort of intro:

Another common technique is to use a tremolo executed by both hands. This tremolo can move or have a short slide, as in the following two examples:

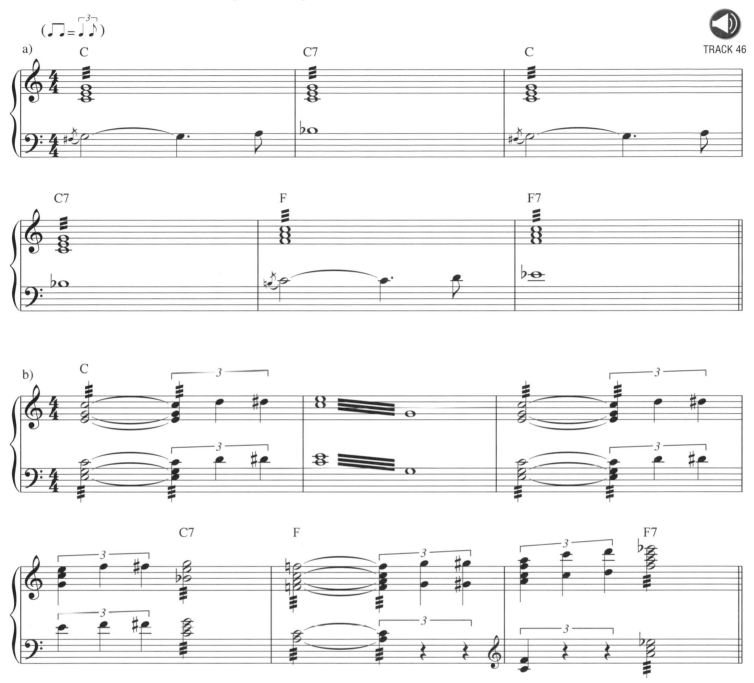

Introductions are free, having neither a set style nor a set number of measures. They rarely employ the bass figure. Usually, when the boogie-woogie bass lines and variations start, they are in marked contrast to the introduction.

Turnarounds and Endings

A turnaround is a two-measure phrase used to lead back to the top of the 12-bar blues. The turnaround occurs in measures 11 and 12 of the form and usually ends on a dominant 7th chord. There are a number of standard turnarounds used in blues. However, boogie-woogie generally doesn't use these turnarounds. Instead, measures 11 and 12 usually continue on the tonic chord. Measure 11 often contains a variation of the crossover right-hand lick or other melodic material.

On the other hand, most endings in boogie-woogie are modified turnarounds, taken straight from the blues. An ending always finishes on the tonic chord. Often, the tonic chord is in dominant 7th form. Our first two-measure ending idea uses a descending walking bass line to connect between the I, the V7, and the I chords. It is in the key of C major:

TRACK 47

If we add some chords to this, we have a Fats Domino style ending phrase. This is a stock blues and boogie-woogie ending. Note that, in the ending sequence, the bass line generally switches to a quarter-note pattern rather than eighth notes:

TRACK 48

An alternative ending is to use an ascending walking bass line:

TRACK 49

We can put two ideas together by using the ascending bass line and putting the descending bass line in the top voice of the right hand. This results in another stock blues ending:

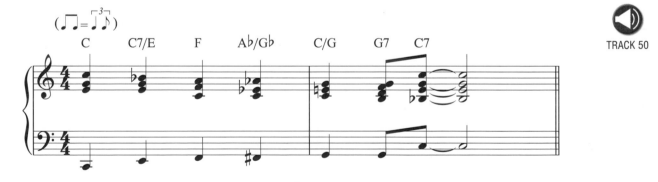

TRACK 50

Here are two possible boogie-woogie endings that use either the ascending or descending walking bass line:

TRACK 51

"Honky Tonk Train Blues" has a different kind of ending – a diminuendo and slow ritard over the last six measures, as if the train is slowing down and coming to a stop.

Breaks

A break is when the bass line stops and other material, often similar to or identical to the intro, is played. Breaks occur at the beginning of a chorus and usually last four to six measures. The following is a break beginning with a two-hand tremolo for one measure, melodic material in quarter-note triplets over the C7 chord for two measures, and then a C9♯5 chord in the final measure:

TRACK 52

The break in Track 53 is essentially a repeat of a four-measure intro:

TRACK 53

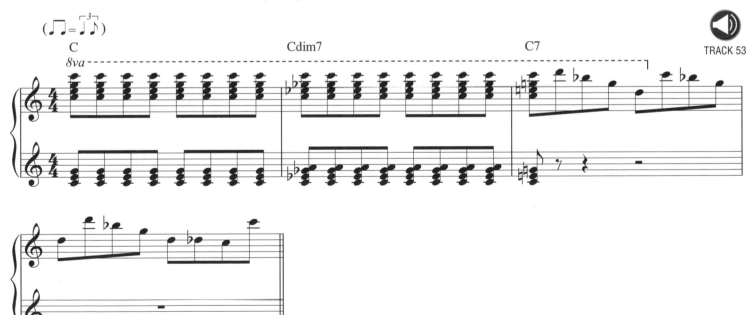

Chapter 11
HOW TO PLAY POPULAR MELODIES IN BOOGIE-WOOGIE STYLE

Any popular tune can be played in boogie-woogie style. The melody is played by the right hand, either in single notes or in chords, while the left hand plays a boogie-woogie bass line that can be chosen from the dozens of common figures.

The chords for the boogie-woogie are indicated by the lead sheet or sheet music of the song. The left-hand bass figures follow the chords of the song.

Probably the most famous boogie-woogie based on a popular song is "Swanee River Boogie," mentioned in Chapter 3. (See page 13.) It has been a featured song in the repertoire of Albert Ammons, Fats Domino, Jools Holland, Dr. John, and pianist/actor Hugh Laurie.

The chords for "Swanee River Boogie" are not a 12-bar blues, but are all I, IV, and V. The bass line is as follows:

TRACK 54

The melody is not played straight, but is executed with swing-style embellishments. These are basically a matter of taste and feel:

TRACK 55

Be selective regarding the song you choose to make a boogie-woogie, because it's easy to cross the boundaries of good taste. That's what happened in the late 1940s, which saw such kitschy compositions as the "Chopsticks Boogie" and "Chopin's Polonaise in Boogie."

Chapter 12

PUTTING IT ALL TOGETHER

We have described all the major elements of boogie-woogie. Now you can combine these when improvising or composing to create your own. Here are some guidelines:

1. Pick a bass line and use it throughout the whole piece. Any bass line can be used with any right-hand part.

2. Pick a version of the 12-bar blues, either with or without the IV chord in measures 2 and 10.

3. Create some melodic material. For example, make up a one-measure riff and try using it with variations through an entire chorus. Create a two-measure phrase and simply repeat it six times in a chorus. Use the techniques of motivic development to vary your riffs. Remember that repetition is inherent in the boogie-woogie style.

4. If you run out of melodic ideas when improvising, play a chordal chorus.

5. Decide how you are going to begin the boogie-woogie. You can start from the top, or play the bass line for a while and then join in, or use an introduction.

6. Figure out how you are going to end the boogie-woogie. Stock endings almost always work.

7. For variety, throw in a break or two. Remember, breaks are often a repeat of the intro

Listen to boogie-woogie recordings or live performances. Try to duplicate bass lines and melodic phrases that you hear. The best way to learn boogie-woogie is by imitation.

Chapter 13
IMPROVISATION IDEAS

In conclusion, here are some general ideas for sparking your creativity and improvisations.

1. **Question and answer.** Ask a question in one phrase and answer it in the next.

2. **Steps and leaps.** Use both in your right hand.

3. **Use repeated notes.** You don't always have to follow a note with a different note.

4. **Leave space (rests) in your music.** It's better to have too little happening than too much.

5. **Play in different registers of the piano.** This is an effective way to change the tone color and texture.

6. **Try using just a few notes** and doing a lot with them, instead of doing very little with lots of notes.

7. **Learn from the masters.** It is a mistake to think that you must reinvent the wheel. In music, as in science, we build on the work of those who have gone before us. All original composers begin with imitation. In borrowing, they develop their craft. Listen to music you enjoy and try to reproduce it on the keyboard. Learn how the music works. This will help imprint the rhythms and structure of effective music into your own hands and brain.

8. **Listen.** Listen to yourself and listen to the masters.

9. **Make mistakes.** Don't be afraid to take risks.

Chapter 14
STYLE FILE

In this chapter we have six examples, each written in the style of a classic boogie-woogie. They show how you can use the basic elements of boogie-woogie to improvise or compose an original song. Each boogie-woogie features an intro, an ending, a break (except "Barrelhouse Rambler Blues") and contains several choruses of the 12-bar blues progression. Some feature a chordal chorus. Each bass line starts and continues throughout the entire piece. Remember to practice the left-hand part alone – slowly to begin with – until it becomes strong, consistent, and automatic.

Each boogie-woogie in the Style File is played twice on the audio, once slowly at the pace of 100 bpm and once at its full speed, either 160 or 170 bpm. If you'd like, play the pieces even faster than indicated.

1. Tree House Boogie-Woogie

Our first tune is written in the style of "Pinetop's Boogie-Woogie" (1928) by Clarence "Pinetop" Smith. It features a six-measure intro using two-hand tremolos, a four-measure break, and a chordal chorus. Set in the key of C, this song uses the 12-bar blues pattern, version two.

The second chorus is based on one of the themes from "Pinetop's Boogie-Woogie." A C crossover lick is used consistently in measure 11 of the 12-bar blues form. Chorus three is based on the famous pattern of 3rds in "Pinetop." Chorus four is chordal, then there is a four-measure break. The fifth chorus features a two-beat riff, while chorus six is a repeat of the second chorus. The piece concludes with a stock ending.

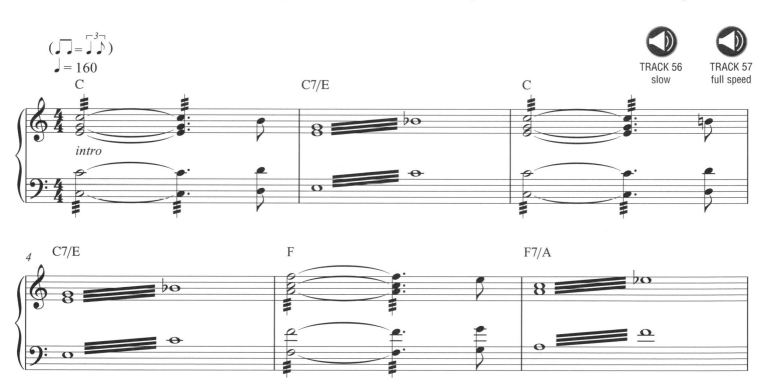

2. Rock 'Em Joe

Next up is an example in the style of "Roll 'Em Pete" (1938) by Pete Johnson, written in the key of C major. It features a four-measure intro, a chordal chorus, and a stock ending. Work on the left-hand part alone until it becomes precise.

The first chorus features 3rds in the right hand, and the second chorus is also based on that same interval. Chorus three is chordal. The fourth chorus employs a lot of repetition featuring 3rds. The lick over the G7 chord is a standard one in boogie-woogie styles.

In the fifth chorus, the right-hand triads are repeated in an eighth-note rhythm in the high register of the piano. This technique foreshadows the rollicking 1950s rock 'n' roll style of Jerry Lee Lewis. Chorus six is a repeat of the second chorus. The tune closes with a stock ending.

TRACK 58
slow

TRACK 59
full speed

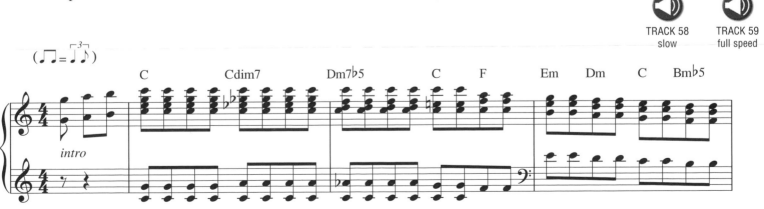

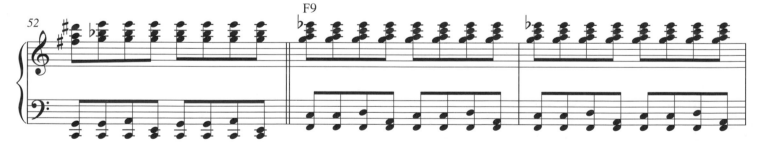

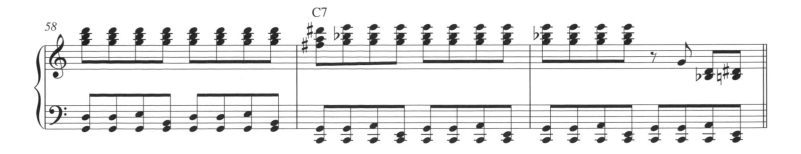

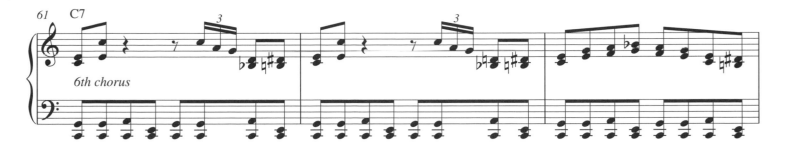

3. The Daily Grind

Our third boogie-woogie is in the style of "Monday Struggle" (1939) by Albert Ammons. It features a four-measure intro, a four-measure break, and a stock ending. It is set in the key of C.

The second chorus is based on a pattern of 6ths. The third chorus features a repeated riff, which is answered by a secondary riff in measures 28 and 32. The fourth chorus features punched chordal rhythms and thirds. The fifth chorus uses patterns based on 3rds. Then there is a four-measure break, which is a repeat of the intro. The ending is a typical one.

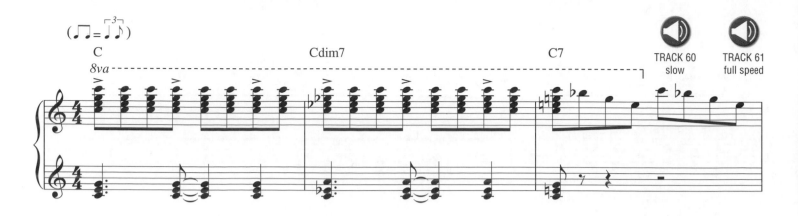

56

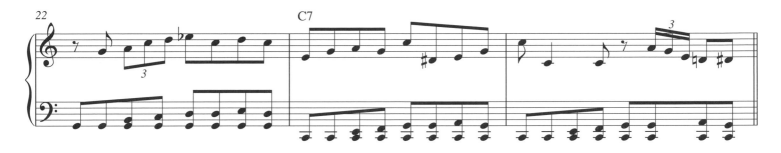

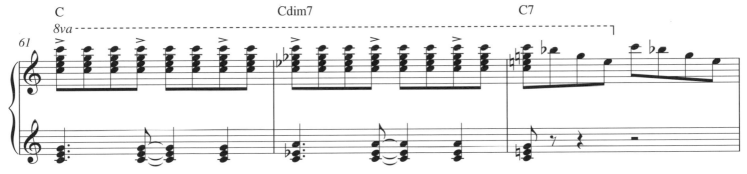

4. Boogie-Woogie I Am

This tune is written in the style of "Boogie-Woogie Be With Me" by German pianist Axel Zwingenberger, who has influenced all of today's boogie-woogie pianists. It features a double-note bass line in the key of G. Work on the left hand alone, slowly at first, until it becomes rhythmically precise.

"Boogie-Woogie I Am" has a four-measure intro. The first chorus is based on a simple five-note riff. The second chorus extends this riff. The third chorus features triplets repeated in the right hand. The break is a repeat of the four-measure intro. The fourth chorus features a two-beat riff. The fifth chorus is based on a new two-measure riff. The sixth chorus is a repeat of chorus one. The ending is routine, except for the sequence of G13 chords in a quarter-note triplet rhythm, which are added to the penultimate measure.

TRACK 62
slow

TRACK 63
full speed

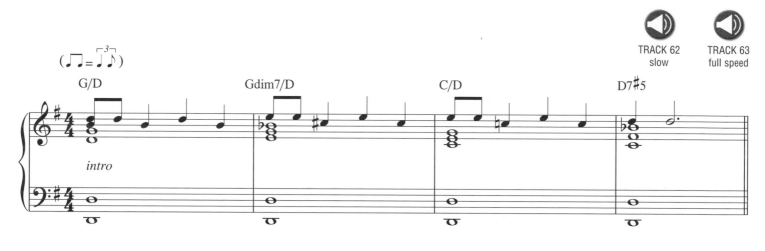

2nd chorus

3rd chorus

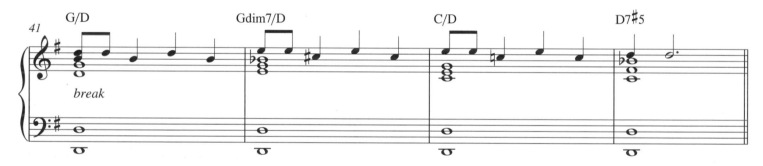

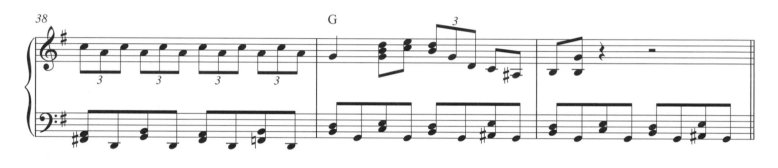

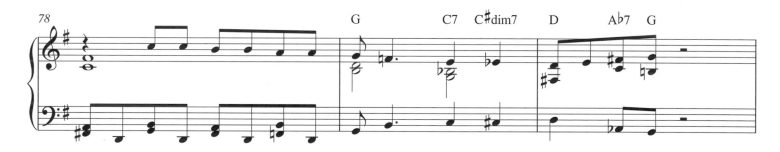

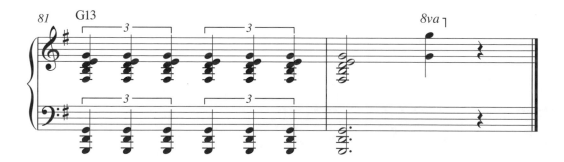

5. Swanee River Boogie

Our next example is in the style of all those pianists who've made it part of their repertoire, including Albert Ammons, Fats Domino, Jools Holland, Dr. John, and actor/pianist Hugh Laurie.

It has no intro. It just starts with the left-hand bass line playing for a bar. It's in the key of C and is divided into 16-measure sections. The first section presents the melody with swing-style embellishments, including lots of grace notes. Parallel 6ths are used in measure 11 and parallel 3rds in measure 16. The bridge begins at measure 18 with parallel 6ths in the right hand.

The entire 32-bar piece is repeated starting at measure 34. Thirds are used again in measures 38–40. The lick over the G chord in measures 56–57 is standard.

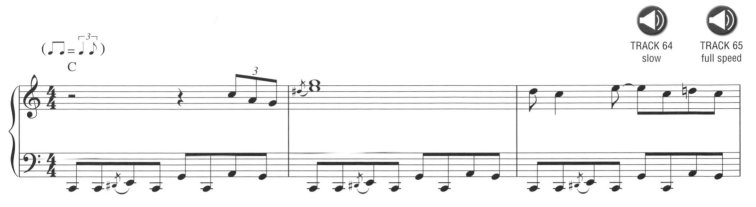

6. Barrelhouse Rambler Blues

This tune is written in the style of "Honky Tonk Train Blues" (1927) by Meade Lux Lewis. It begins with a two-measure intro that uses a two-hand tremolo. It's in the key of G.

The left hand uses a unique chordal bass pattern. It suggests the chugging of a train, while the right hand mimics train whistles and various railroad noises. The piece follows a long tradition of train imitations in boogie-woogie.

The first chorus establishes the pervasive triplet feel. The second chorus sets up a polyrhythm with quarter-note triplets in the right hand against eighth notes in the left hand. There is also an intentional use of dissonance, with the G minor chord in the right hand and the G major chord in the left hand.

The third chorus uses tremolo in the right hand and quarter-note triplets. The fourth chorus employs quarter-note triplets in the right hand against eighth notes in the left hand and tone clusters over the G chord in measure 45. The fifth chorus features a two-beat riff. In general, the last four measures of each chorus are the same.

There is no ending per se. The piece simply ritards like a train slowing down until it stops.

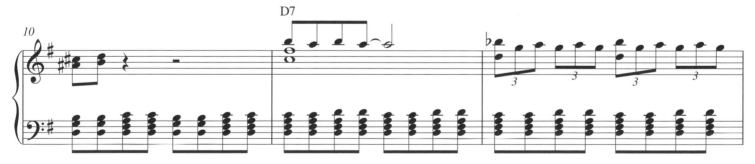

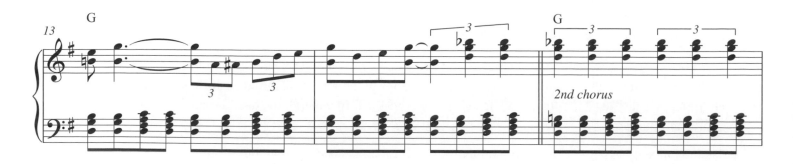

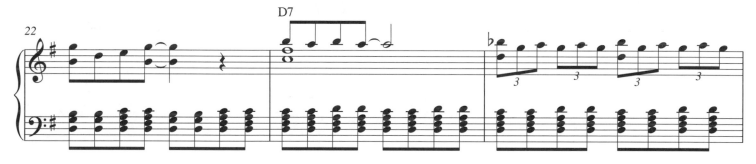

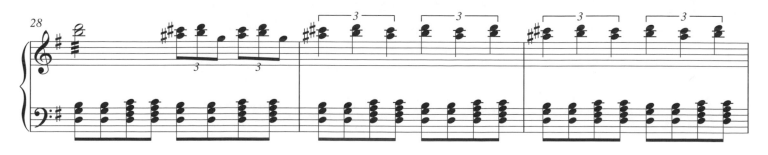

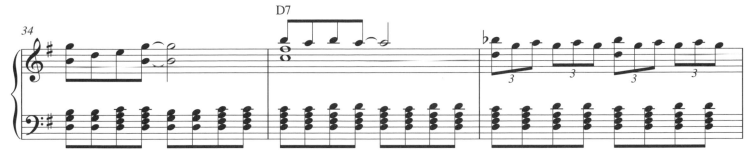

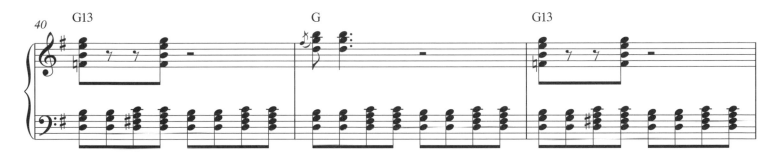

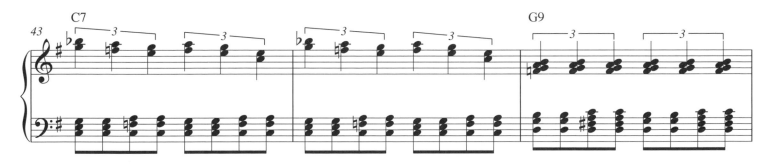

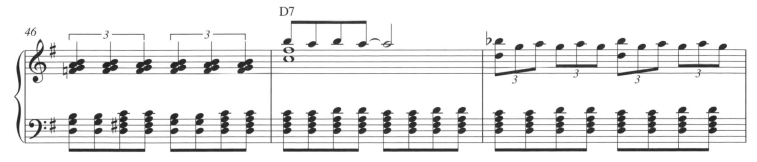

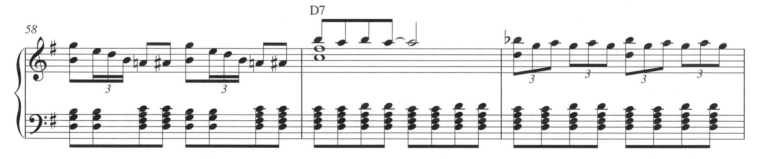

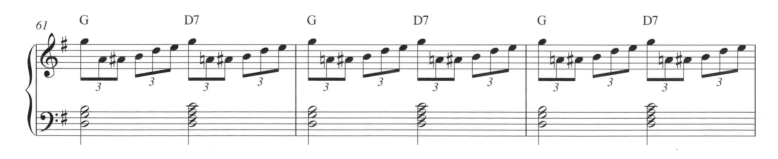

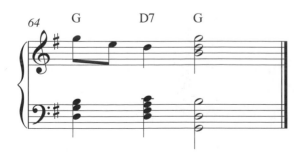